BIRMINGHAM VIEW
THROUGH THE YEARS IN PHOTOGRAPHS

ORIGINAL LIMITED EDITION

ISBN 0-943994-21-7
Library of Congress Number 96-078805
Copyright © 1996
Birmingham Historical Society
One Sloss Quarters
Birmingham, Alabama 35222
Telephone 205-251-1880

COVER ILLUSTRATION:

Theater Row, Second Avenue North between 19th and 20th Streets, 1937, Jimmy Wilson, Birmingham View. This photograph captures the vitality of the city center in the 1930s, when downtown was the primary destination for shopping and entertainment, as well as for business and professional services.

BIRMINGHAM VIEW
THROUGH THE YEARS IN PHOTOGRAPHS

PIERCE LEWIS

MARJORIE LONGENECKER WHITE

EDITOR

PHILIP A. MORRIS

PUBLISHER

BIRMINGHAM HISTORICAL SOCIETY

Studios, 416 21st St. North, 1910. During his career, J. Frank Knox owned two photographic studios: Birmingham View, the commercial studio he ran from 1906 to 1910 (and with which he was associated into the 1920s), and Knox Studio, a portrait studio he set up in 1910 and operated until 1973. Stopping by the two studios is the Rev. James ("Brother") Bryan, pastor to Third Presbyterian Church on Southside and beloved preacher whose compassion extended to people throughout the industrial city. The young photographer could have no better endorsement for his ventures than that of Brother Bryan.

INTRODUCTION

Where old photographs of Birmingham hang on the wall, most of us stop to look at the moment the camera captured. We look for information, clues about people and places and how the city once looked and people lived.

Established in 1871, Birmingham is young enough that all of its history was subject to photographic record. The Birmingham Public Library Archives has approximately 200,000 photographs in its possession. That number has gone up appreciably with the recent gift of some 14,000 negatives by Gary and Jackie Dobbs, all the work of one of the city's longtime commercial photography studios, Birmingham View. The gift prompted this publication and its name. "Birmingham View" derives from the type of equipment the photographer used: a "view camera" so named because the photographer composes and studies a full-sized image (view) on the ground glass of the tripod camera before exposing the film.

The Birmingham View Company operated from c.1905 until 1961 in the heart of the Birmingham city center, providing commissioned images for clients, not for speculation or for pleasure. Birmingham View had no intention of leaving behind a comprehensive record of Birmingham's history during the first half of the 20th century. Quite accidentally, however, it did leave behind an unusually broad view of the city, during the time of its most explosive growth. Birmingham View was paid mainly to record scenes of commercial Birmingham, as well as photographs of official gatherings and various public events. In the process, and this is what is remarkable about the collection, the studio also captured much of the flavor of Birmingham as it was converted from a kind of adolescent industrial newcomer on the Southern urban scene to a large mature city, one of the few big industrial cities in a largely non-industrial South. In effect, this remarkable collection of photographs catches Birmingham by surprise, in the process of becoming a city.

Research to date has not revealed exactly how the Birmingham View Company operated in its earliest years. Brothers Edgar J. and George R. Hilty, then also employed in managerial positions at The First National Bank and Republic Iron and Steel Corporation, worked with the company by 1905. A year later, J. Frank Knox, upon discovering that his camera views of locomotives sold quite well, made photography his life long career. For the next five years, he recorded diverse city scenes, nearly always with engaging views of people in an urban context. In 1910, he also opened a portrait studio where he photographed the faces of Birmingham until 1973. Auburn University Archives in Auburn, Alabama now owns the well indexed collection of 35,361 Knox Portrait Studio negatives. In 1923, Knox sold Birmingham View to George M. D. Davis. That studio prospered in the late 1920s. Birmingham city directory advertisements state the company motto: "We Photograph Anything, Any Where, Any Time . . . Views, Groups, Banquets and Commercial Photography." Copying, enlarging and framing were also part of the studio service.

Among the photographers working and freelancing for Birmingham View from 1927 to 1937 were German born Richard Herschell; Ernest Pryor, a staff photographer for Tennessee, Coal and Iron Company (TCI); Walter Rosser, a *Birmingham News* photographer; Jimmy Wilson, later a portrait photographer; Mercer Wilson who had been previously associated with the Stephenson Studio, an upscale portrait studio; and Fred Arthur Powell.

Fred Arthur Powell acquired the studio in 1929 and operated it until 1961. Powell continued to photograph until his death in 1975. Gary Dobbs acquired the studio negatives dating from the 1920s from Powell's widow. The eight-by-ten-inch negative format was discontinued in the early 1940s, thus forming a cut off point for image selection for this publication. The studio's four-by-five inch negatives were made with portable, hand-held cameras. All negatives had been stacked in drawers, at random, with clients and years listed sometimes on the negatives and sometimes on the tattered negative sleeves. Gary Dobbs and his wife Jackie, who worked with both "Mr. Knox" and Jimmy Wilson, inventoried, categorized and began identifying the vast collection.

To round out the years included in this publication (principally, the first half of the 20th century) and include representative work of other Birmingham-based studios of the era, this publication also presents images by F. A. Cloud, Cloud Studio (active 1918-32); Bert

Fred Arthur Powell with his Studio Camera, 1940s. Photographer Fred Powell supervised the Birmingham View studio for more than four decades. Some 14,000 8-by-10 and 4-by-5-inch negatives, dating from the 1920s to the 1960s, were in the company files at his death. They comprise the Birmingham View collection acquired by Gary and Jackie Dobbs and recently donated to the Birmingham Public Library Archives for public use and enjoyment.

G. Covell, Covell's Studio (active 1901-16); O. V. (Oscar) Hunt (active 1917-54); and A.C. Keily (active 1914-57). A view by John T. Horgan, Jr., Horgan Photo (active 1890-93), one of 5,000 photographs he made of the city and environs, sets the stage for the city's phenomenal growth.

Although there are many artful compositions on these pages, this is not intended to be a book of art photography. These are photographs of record, most taken for commercial or institutional clients. They would have been put to many different uses. But for us today they serve to reveal the past. And often it is not the stated subject alone we find instructive, but all the details that were simply part of the scene. For example, the World War I era Red Cross nurses are lined up for a formal portrait, but the eye discovers the boys behind playing hoops in what is now Linn Park.

Legends that describe, as best we can determine, what the photographs show have been researched in primary sources and written by Marjorie White with assistance from the staffs of the Birmingham Historical Society and Birmingham Public Library Archives, Southern History and Government Documents Departments, as well as volunteers who have drawn on personal research and memories to provide clues to the "history mysteries" posed by the pictures.

To give this local photographic record a sense of perspective, we called on a friend, Pierce Lewis, professor emeritus of geography at Pennsylvania State University. After reviewing our selection of photographs, he selected several to illuminate with brief essays. It was Dr. Lewis who encouraged Birmingham Historical Society to proceed with the publication project, feeling the city's rapid growth from frontier to metropolitan status in such a brief span of time would come through clearly in these photographs. And with his career focus on cultural geography, whose purpose is discovering the telling truths that emanate from daily life, he helped us see what the photographs reveal.

The images are arranged in rough chronology. There are no over-riding themes or categories. And very many of them might be described as ordinary, not earth-shaking or even Birmingham-shaking. But it is precisely the non-dramatic but faithful documentation of city life over the years that we think you may enjoy. The photographs invite repeated study: a bemusing and often surprising walk through the decades.

BIRMINGHAM VIEW
THROUGH THE YEARS IN PHOTOGRAPHS

20th Street, Looking North from Powell Avenue to Capitol (now Linn) Park, with the L & N Passenger Station and Shed, left, 1890, J.T. Horgan, Jr. Twenty years after its founding in 1871, Birmingham was the main city of the North Alabama mineral region, with a commercial core of three- and four-story brick offices and stores extending from the railroad tracks to Third Avenue North. Horse-drawn wagons and streetcars transported people and goods through the early city's wide dirt streets.

Volunteers Leaving for the Spanish American War, 20th St. Looking South from Morris Avenue, Sunday, May 1, 1898, Photographer Unknown. Answering an April 22 call to serve their nation, 700 North Alabama recruits are boarding a special train at the Birmingham station. Well-wishers, protected from the sun with hats and parasols, bid them adieu, packing the station shed (where the train will soon pull in for loading) and spilling onto 20th Street. The patriotic fervor has curtailed streetcar service, electrified since 1891. The war was over before many of these Southerners made it to Cuba.

Fittings Foundry, American Cast Iron Pipe Company (ACIPCO), c.1908, Birmingham View 481. Posing as molten iron is poured into vertical molds, these men were among the thousands who found employment in the city's growing manufacturing industries. By 1908, the Birmingham District had become a leading center of iron and pipemaking. Such local companies as ACIPCO, Beggs, Dimmick, Southern, Stockham and the forerunners of U. S. Pipe and Foundry Company were producing pipe for waste and water transmission and selling it in fast-growing urban areas nationwide.

3898

Slag Heaps, Unidentified Location, c.1908, Bert G. Covell. Since the beginning of large-scale ironmaking in the 1880s, mountains of slag, a waste-product of pig iron manufacture, had been accumulating at area furnace works. Making iron from Birmingham ores produced one ton of slag per ton of pig iron. Birmingham companies crushed the slag and sold it as street paving, railroad ballast, soil conditioner and road construction material. Birmingham-based Vulcan Materials Company, a Fortune 500 corporation, got its start selling slag.

Entry, St. Mary's-on-the-Highlands Episcopal Church (1892), 12th Ave. and 19th St. South, Early 1900s, Birmingham View. Prominent industrialists were among the charter members of St. Mary's Church, built on the Highlands, as the hills south of the city were known, removed from the heat and noise of the sooty industrial plants in the city center. During the late 1880s, the city's building boom attracted European-trained designers and craftsmen, including architect John Sutcliffe. Sutcliffe designed this English Gothic-style church, built of Kansas sandstone, pictured here framed by poplars and planted with ivy.

Drawing Room, Library and Dining Room, Unidentified Residence, c.1908, Birmingham View 763. The occupants of this house seem to enjoy collecting worldly goods. The walls are decked with stencilled decorations, the floors with Oriental rugs and the cabinets and bookcase with porcelains, cut-glass vases and artfully arranged bric-a-brac. The furniture includes Victorian, Colonial Revival and Craftsman pieces. Chairs, cushions, tables and two writing desks pack the columned interiors.

Bouquet of Belles, Munger House, 11th Ave. and 19th St. South, 1909, Birmingham View 3293. Cotton gin manufacturer and inventor Robert Munger owned some of the first automobiles in the city. After specifying elements of their design, he imported two Wintons and a Panhard from Europe. This photograph records one of these autos with floral decorations and his son and daughters brilliantly attired in lacy day dresses, bonnets and parasols. A neighbor's family scrapbook described the occasion as an "auto parade" accented by dazzlingly beautiful and, presumably, marriageable belles!

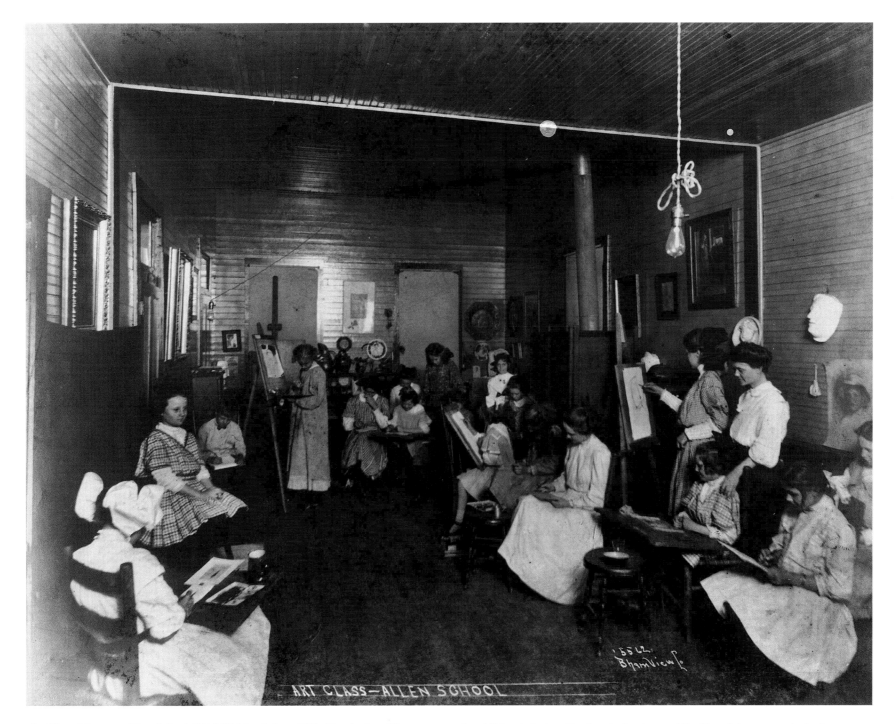

ART CLASS—ALLEN SCHOOL

Art Class, Margaret Allen School, 2144 Highland Ave., 1909, Birmingham View 5562. Well-dressed young women and a young boy develop their artistic skills sketching and painting water colors of their classmate (left). Plaster casts and framed art works hang on the walls of the studio, lit by a dangling electric light.

In addition to instruction in art, dancing and the French language, students attending this private girls' school received solid grounding in the three Rs. Principal Miss Willie M. Allen, together with her spinster sisters Beff and Ruth, ran the Allen School from 1906 to 1934.

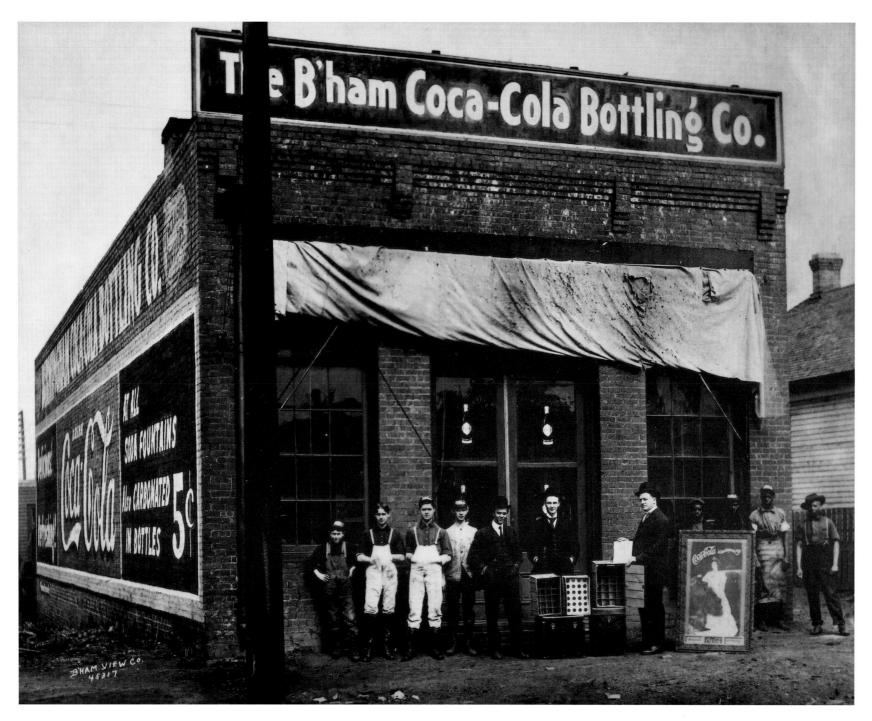

The Birmingham Coca-Cola Bottling Co., 1708 Ave. B (now Second Ave. South), c.1907, Birmingham View 45317. In 1899, Chattanooga businessmen acquired the U.S. bottling rights for Coca-Cola from Asa Candler of Atlanta. Not long after, they began selling franchises for the drink that had been invented for soda fountains and first bottled in 1894. In 1902, Crawford Johnson, Sr., (fifth from left) acquired the rights to bottle coke in the Birmingham area with the Chattanooga firm furnishing syrup and sweetener. This crew mixed the syrup with carbonated water, bottled the Coca-Cola and shipped it via wagon and rail in 15- and 24-bottle cases.

Baptism, Unidentified Location, c.1910, Birmingham View 12246. Friends and relatives, protecting themselves from the heat and a light rain, have gathered on the lawn and open porches of this turn-of-the-century cottage to witness the baptism of the indivduals pictured partially immersed in a creek or pond. Such open-air baptisms were common in the rural communities surrounding Birmingham until the early 1950s.

Street Workers with Guards, 100 Block 24th St. North, August 10, 1909, Birmingham View 6141. As was common in American cities of this era, private businesses handled many basic city services including garbage collection, mass transportation, gas, electricity and water delivery. Birmingham city government did employ firemen and policemen, and from 1897 to 1910, it used convicts to clean and repair streets and sewers. Persons convicted of crimes such as vagrancy, larceny and assault and battery who could not pay their fines were sentenced to chain gangs. In 1909, approximately 190 men served on street crews each day. These laborers use pickaxes to dig up the street for repaving.

Salvation Army Wagon, Unidentified Location Downtown, 1908, Birmingham View 2574. Men pose with waste paper collected from downtown stores and offices, while uniformed drivers waiting with their carriages look on. Established in the city by 1900, the Salvation Army's "industrial home" and store was a self-supporting opera- tion that mingled a ministry of spiritual regeneration with the opportunity to work. The army offered unemployed men shelter for three- to four-weeks and jobs baling waste paper and repairing furniture and clothing collected from citizens for resale to the needy.

The Women's Christian Temperance Union (WCTU) was an organization of mostly Protestant women who banded together during the late 19th century to oppose the consumption of alcoholic beverages and to lobby for laws prohibiting the manufacture and sale of alcoholic beverages. In 1919, a decade after this photograph was taken, these well-dressed women and their numerous allies would succeed at the national level as the U. S. Congress and three-quarters of all state legislatures passed the Prohibition Amendment to the U. S. Constitution.

In 1933, with the repeal of national prohibition, many people concluded that prohibition was a failure and derided the WCTU as a band of silly fanatics. That view overlooks some grim history. Alcohol abuse in early 20th century America was far worse than anything we know today. The prohibition movement was a reaction to the widespread abuse of alcohol which had grown rapidly worse with the growth of cities and industry. Many people quite reasonably believed that alcohol abuse was destroying not just the bodies and souls of individuals, but their families and society at large. These women's reaction may have been extreme, but so was their provocation. *P.L.*

East Lake Park, c.1909, Birmingham View 4999. During the late 1880s, real estate speculators routinely bought farmland on the city's edges, converted the land into residential building lots and extended streetcar lines to connect the newly formed suburbs to the city's commercial and industrial core. To promote the 2,000-acre East Lake subdivision as "an ideal pleasure resort," developers created this 33-acre lake, built modest frame cottages and arranged a steady schedule of open-air concerts, vaudeville shows and novel and daring acts. This man balances atop a five-story frame tower set in the lake.

WCTU Campaign for Prohibition, Near an Unidentified Polling Place, November 29, 1909, Birmingham View 6836. This group, called "White Ribboners" for the white ribbons they wear in support of their mission to ban drinking, is gathered on the day of a vote to amend the Alabama constitution to outlaw the use and sale of alcoholic beverages. The women did not have the vote, but they did have the influence. Two years earlier, Jefferson County went dry and saloon and brewery doors had closed. Ebullient with that success, the ladies sought to put Alabama on the "arid" list, setting an early example for national prohibition legislation.

Evening Banquet, Unidentified Location, 1909, Birmingham View 6180. A group of young men are gathered to dine, perhaps in a downtown hotel. Waiters, dressed in three-piece cutaways, pose with diners, adding to the clubbiness and formality of this portrait. The table is set for a multi-course meal with the starter courses of fruit cocktail, sliced tomatoes and crackers. Olives and grape leaves form the centerpieces. Breezes circulate through open, lace-curtained windows and transoms over the doors. Hanging gas fixtures, converted to electricity, provide illumination.

Hooper's Cafe, 312-314 20th St. North, Opening Day, February, 1906, Birmingham View. Well-located on the city's main street, near both commercial and residential districts, this eatery was run by brothers Clint and John Hooper until the Depression. Pressed metal panels ornament the ceiling and landscape murals grace the walls.

Light switches operate the fanciful ceiling lights and whirling overhead fans circulating air. Men eat at the counter while ladies and their escorts dine at the linen-clad tables. Ketchup and hot sauce accompany meals, with pies for dessert and cigars for sale at the cash register.

Christmas Sale, Post Card Exchange, 1822 Second Ave. North, 1909, Birmingham View 4498. William H. Faulkner ran this and similar stores in the city center from 1909 until 1946, offering shoppers the opportunity to tour the world via cards and trinkets. Only in a thriving "big city" could such a high degree of specialized retailing prosper. Flamboyant hanging fixtures and bulbs lining the vaulted ceiling and side mirrors provide illumination for post cards displayed on the racks and counters. Potted palms and ferns, paper decorations and a small Christmas tree complete the exotic setting enjoyed by male shoppers.

Empire Building, 20th St. at First Ave. North, June 17, 1909, Birmingham View 5755. Birmingham's skyline climbed to 16-stories as this skyscraper office building rose during 1909. Birmingham View documented its construction monthly. Foundations were set by January 15, the first column of the top tier of structural steel was in place three months later. By May 15, the exterior terra cotta block had been mortared and anchored. And by mid-June, the building was nearly finished. Teams of expert craftsmen, using limited machinery, hand carried the construction materials needed to build the tower. The 1910 city directory indicates the city's newest skyscraper filled quickly with tenants who worked in industry, insurance, mortgages, real estate and lumber.

Five Points Circle, 20th St. at 11th Ave. South, c.1912, A. C. Keily 1060. This view looks north across the "highland" plateau toward the valley in which the city's commercial and industrial districts are concentrated. Arriving from the city center via the 20th Street Hill, a streetcar approaches the Five Points Circle. Here, riders load, unload and enjoy the lively surroundindgs. Their presence contributes to the success of neighborhood businesses. Early commercial buildings conform to the contours of the circle. The large buildings (right) are South Highlands School and the exuberantly styled Highlands Methodist Church (1909).

RED MOUNTAIN.

Red Mountain View, 1909, Birmingham View 5314. This newly surfaced "all-weather" road traverses the southern flank of Red Mountain. (All-weather meant the surface had been treated and one wouldn't bog down in the mud!) Shades Mountain, heavily forested and totally undeveloped, looms on the far horizon. Electric power lines extend to a site at the crest of the ridge. A single pedestrian and a carriage use the road which, 30 years later, with curves removed, became the route of U. S. 31, passing over the mountain along 20th Street South at Vulcan Park, whence it descended into the Rosedale and Homewood neighborhoods and on to Montgomery.

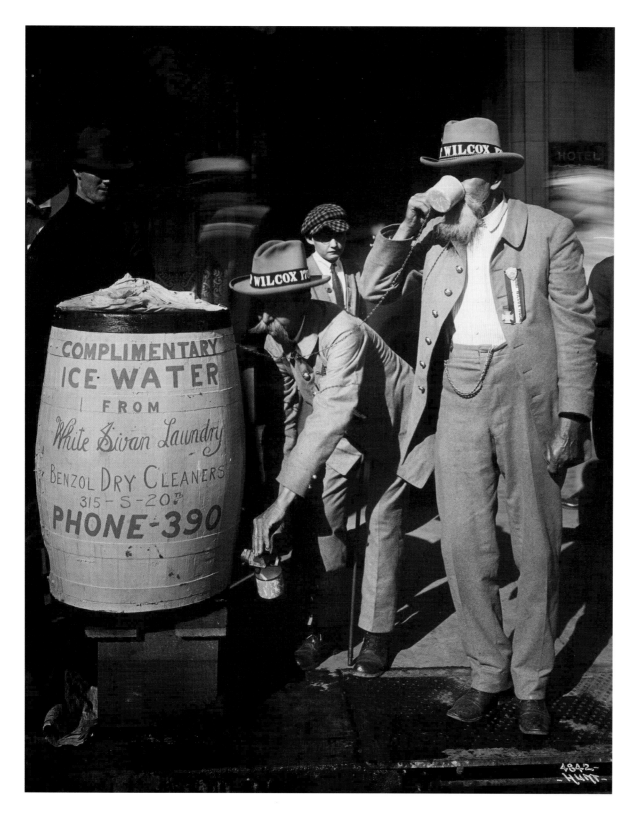

The electric streetcar was a powerful instrument for urban change in America, and it helps explain the spread-out geographic shape of America's industrial cities, including Birmingham.

Before the time of the streetcar, cities and towns were geographically compact. They had to be, since most city people had no choice but to walk from one place to another. Consequently, workers lived close to factories or mines, or over the shops where they worked, often in very crowded quarters. Only the affluent could afford horses and buggies for commuting to far-off suburbs.

The streetcar changed all that. Light in weight and driven by the newly invented direct current electric motor, streetcars could move at high speeds, yet could start and stop quickly. Now, masses of people could move quickly and cheaply from workplaces in one part of the city to residences which could be located almost anywhere, so long as they were near a trolley line. Factories like American Steel and Wire Mill could sprawl over huge areas in one part of the urban area, while workers could live in residential neighborhoods elsewhere. Those neighborhoods might also sprawl considerably since streetcar stops could be spaced at close intervals and could be located anywhere along the line. The arrangement permitted cities like Birmingham and its suburbs to occupy huge areas, vastly larger than traditional old-world cities. The trolley at the right is headed for downtown Birmingham and, then, for suburban East Lake more than 17 miles away. *P.L.*

Confederate Veterans' Parade, May 16, 1916, O. V. Hunt. From 1890 to 1932, Confederate veterans and their sons and daughters reunited annually in cities across the South. Host cities (Birmingham in 1894, 1908, 1916 and 1926) organized private entertainments and public festivities, featuring immense parades. Birmingham's 1916 parade drew an estimated 100,000 spectators. Six thousand veterans wearing their well-worn uniforms with memorial crosses and 10,000 sons, daughters, grandchildren and others participated. Along the parade route, businesses set up relief stations offering ice water. These veterans served with Major General Cadmus M. Wilcox in many campaigns of the army of Northern Virginia.

Shift Change, American Steel and Wire Mill Co., Valley Avenue, Fairfield, 1916, Birmingham View 13092. Streetcars wait outside the landscaped entrance to the general offices of this United States Steel subsidiary. From 1914 to 1979, the mill operated at this site, producing wire of various guages, barbed wire, woven wire fence, nails, staples and rods and providing jobs for approximately 1,200 workers. At the time of this photograph, Birmingham's streetcar system had 250 miles of track, making it one of the largest street railway systems in the United States, with a ridership estimated at 135,000 per day.

Sipsey Mine, Sipsey, December 12, 1913, O. V. Hunt 2342. Mine workers pose amidst the newly opened surface operations at this Walker County mine. The bridge (right rear) leads across the Sipsey River. On both sides of the river, drift mines open 30-inch seams of high-quality, easily accessible steam coal. The mined coal was washed, sized, loaded into railcars and shipped, principally to railroads. In 1914, 400 persons worked at this mine and produced 245,831 tons of coal, more than any other mine in the county. Operations at the locally owned Sipsey mine remained strong into the late 1930s.

Company Housing, Sipsey, December 12, 1913, O.V. Hunt 2337. The village at Sipsey consisted of a large commissary, school buildings, a church and 200 four-room, pyramidal-roof houses erected with lumber sawn at the site. Long-leaf pine, dried in the sun and finished by company planers, provided dressed lumber for interior use. This village was located on flat farm land and laid out in streets and avenues. In 1913, the four-room houses rented for $6.00 a month. Mine workers made between $1.50 and $3.00 for a 10-hour day. Flour cost 75 cents per 24-pound sack. Many company buildings, remodelled over the years, remain at Sipsey, today.

Fire, Birmingham Railway, Light and Power Co. General Offices, First Ave. North at 21st St., May 8, 1914, Birmingham View 19206. On this afternoon, workers departing their offices witnessed this "veritable inferno of flames. . .brick walls standing without support," as the *Birmingham Age-Herald* reported the fire which consumed the headquarters of the private firm that provided the city's gas and electric power and ran its street railways. On the same site, the company built a new office tower, cladding its exterior with fire-retardant, terra cotta sheathing. The tower remains and is now named Landmark Center.

Beehive Coke Ovens, possibly TCI Coal Mines, Blocton, c.1912, O. V. Hunt 110.
Fires burn to convert coal to coke, the fuel for making iron and steel. Before widespread use of by-product processes, by which ammonium and other gases are contained and used, coke was made in these structures called "beehive" ovens because of their shape. The "dinky" engineer loads coal into the ovens, which burns for about 48 hours at which point laborers open the brick oven doors and rake out the hot coke, still smoking with hot sulphurous fumes. The ovens are then rebricked and reloaded. The dinky takes the coke to the blast furnaces or railhead.

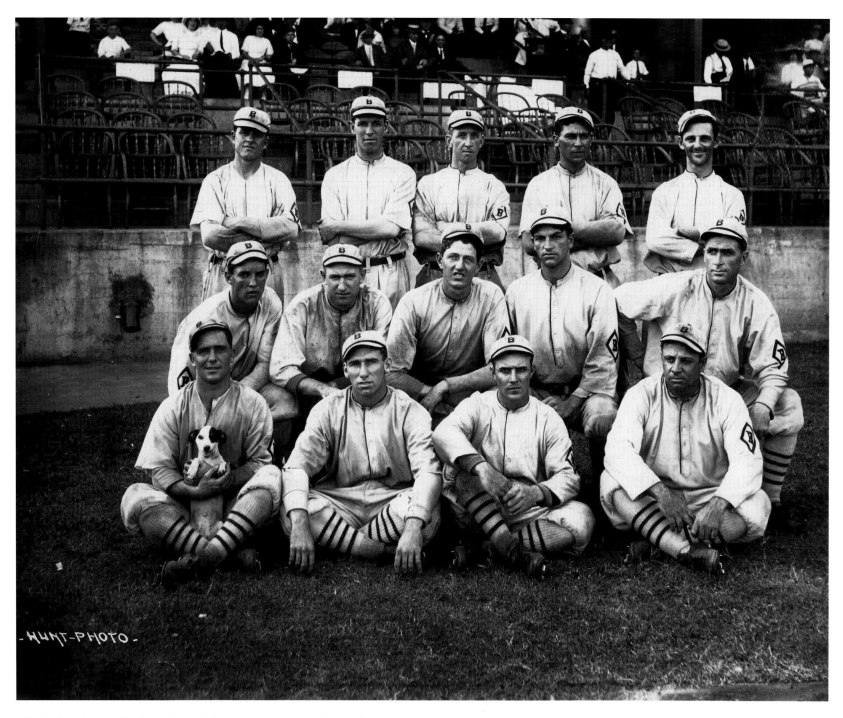

Birmingham Barons Baseball Team, Rickwood Field, Spring, 1917, O. V. Hunt 1194. Southern League pennant winners in 1912 and 1914, the Birmingham Barons also claimed title to the finest ballpark in the minor leagues. Birminghamians played and supported baseball and so did the Barons' enthusiastic owner, Rick Woodward, a local ironmaking mogul whose family had built this grandstand seven years before the photograph was made. Wooden spectator chairs fill the infield boxes. Today, America's oldest standing ballpark hosts more than 250 baseball games, annually, as well as movie filmings and visitors.

"Tiling a Field," Fairfield, 1910s, Bert Covell. A surveyor uses a level to establish proper elevations for laying pipe to drain this swampy land while a laborer helps to adjust the level in the ditch. The drainage pipe sections are made of terra cotta tile. At this time, the industrial center at Corey (later Fairfield), just west of Birmingham, was being developed. The Tennessee Coal and Iron Company (TCI) Health Department, under the direction of Dr. Lloyd Noland, drained and treated nearby swamps to reduce the incidence of malaria and typhoid and to prepare the land for subdivision.

Gaines Grocery Co., 2700 Ave. F (now Sixth) South, c.1916, O. V. Hunt 4887.
Providing and delivering fresh meats (the chickens are still alive in the sidewalk coop) and groceries to residents along Highland Avenue are Charles Gaines and his staff. This photograph features a new motorized delivery cycle fitted with a headlight and spatter-protected wheel guards. Its driver is located in a low sitting position, thereby reducing wind resistance. This cycle must have made the daily delivery drudge a breeze. In 1916, the city directory lists some 712 independent grocers and no supermarkets or chain stores.

Birmingham Police Bicycle Force, 419 19th St. North, c.1916. A group of 20 police-men sport new bicycles, presumably purchased at Edwards Cycle Store, adjacent to City Hall, then located on 19th Street. Since the 1880s, bicycle manufacturers had urged use of their machines by the army, the post office, messengermen and police-men. Specially trained policemen, they claimed, might overtake and apprehend both pedestrians and motorists. Next to the cycle shop is Mayer Brothers, an establish-ment run by Joseph, Samuel, Albert and Harry Mayer. Opened in 1898, Mayer's sold wallpaper, pictures, frames and interior decorating services for six decades.

Faculty, Cunningham School, 4307 Eighth Ave. North, 1912, Birmingham View. In 1910, Birmingham annexed many surrounding municipalities and grew from a city of 11.4 square miles to 48.3 square miles and from 38,415 people to 132,685 people, making it the fourth largest city in the South after New Orleans, Louisville and Atlanta.

The annexation doubled the school-age population and added 40 schools to the city system. Although many of these schools were substandard, East Birmingham's Cunningham School was built of brick and its doors equipped with a new invention, "panic bars" for speedy exits.

Alabama Boys' Industrial School New Year's Day Outing, Unidentified Cafe, January 1, 1915, Birmingham View 14757. Beneath the watchful eyes of many chaperones, white-jacketed waiters have set cafe tables and the soda fountain with a banquet for these 75 boys. At the right with the cafe's proprietors are Col. David Weakly, the school's director and, wearing a hat reflecting her social prominence, Mrs. R. D. Johnston, the crusading civic leader who conceived, financed and organized her female friends to sustain this reform school for delinquent boys. Established in 1900 by the state legislature, it is now the Vacca Campus of the Alabama Department of Youth Services.

Red Cross Nurses, Capitol (now Linn) Park, Saturday, May 10, 1919, Birmingham View 18340. With thousands cheering, Birmingham welcomed home its World War I heroines and heroes. A grand Victory Parade through gaily festooned streets disbanded in Capitol Park, where participants were briefly reunited with their loved ones and then whisked off to other celebrations. Local women, who had organized a Red Cross chapter in 1909, greatly expanded their efforts during World War I. While Birmingham nurses served abroad, 4,000 ladies across the city sewed, knitted and made surgical dressings for war victims.

Participants, 26th Annual Confederate Veterans' Reunion, Tutwiler Hotel Lobby, May 1916, Birmingham View 49026. Visitor accommodations included several hotels for high-ranking former officers and tents at the Fairgrounds for the rank and file. Boy Scouts escorted visitors about the city. According to a *Birmingham News* account, black veterans, most of whom served both as bodyguards and as enlisted soldiers bearing muskets, were "being well cared for and treated as their faithfulness deserves." Convening at The Tutwiler at the same time are advocates for improved roads and air travel.

Typing Class, Massey Business College, 2024 Third Ave. North, c.1924, Birmingham View 23564. One of several business colleges in the city, Prof. Richard Massey's private school taught by doing. Students learned business skills by conducting real life transactions. Graduates achieved positions as bookkeepers, stenographers and managers. This photograph shows 56 well-dressed students seated at individual desks, with paper supply and trash sacks at their right, practicing typing on Remington typewriters. Blackboard charts track performance. This building still stands today. The business school has closed.

This scene along 20th Street depicts Birmingham on the boundary between the old and the new. The low buildings to the left were typical of 18th and 19th century American small town main streets, with small mom-and-pop shops on the street level. The second floor was commonly residential, often occupied by the shop-owner and his family. The shops' patrons lived nearby. The entire arrangement was small-scale and relatively unsophisticated.

The First National Bank Building represents the arrival of a modern urban order. The high concentration of office workers, all in one building, required mass transportation to bring them from outlying residential locations. The building itself required modern technology, too. Without steel girders (which form the building's structural skeleton) and high-speed elevators to reach the upper floors, such buildings could not function. *P.L.*

First National Bank (now Frank Nelson) Building, Looking South on 20th St. Towards Drennen Co. (department store) and the Rear of the Brown Marx Building at First Ave. North, c.1920, Birmingham View 23734. It is 4:15 one afternoon and everyone (their names painted on the windows or lettered on the buildings or in projecting signs) is still at work. In these pre-air-conditioning days, awnings are out and windows open with curtains blowing in the breeze. This office building, completed in 1904, was Class A office space. The city's leading banking institution, First National Bank, occupies the first floor. Other tenants include 184 individuals and 48 firms, many of them two- or three-attorney legal firms. The Birmingham Bar Association library is housed on the 11th floor. The city's visionary real estate firm, Jemison Co., has a streetfront entrance. Jemison had already developed major buildings downtown, the industrial city of Fairfield, Forest Park and would later develop Redmont and Mountain Brook.

East End Cafe and Ryan Harness Co. Manufacturers, 109-11 24th St. North, c.1927, Birmingham View 45317. Well into the 1920s, the city center retained small town functions and scale, with independent family businesses filling many 25-foot shopfronts with lively offerings. The East End Cafe, a homey spot with sweet peas growing in window boxes, served dinners for 25 cents. A 1914 City ordinance required separate entrances and service for "colored" and "white" customers. Next door, the Ryan brothers made harnesses for patrons who still used horse-drawn vehicles, their numbers diminishing throughout the decade.

Excelsior Steam Laundry Co. Building, 1807 Second Ave. North, 1924, Birmingham View 26653. The sooty industrial city supported the establishment of several large laundries including the Excelsior Laundry, opened in 1887. Two years later, proprietors George A. Blinn and George A. Blinn, Jr., built this distinctively corbelled brick laundry where they steam-cleaned clothes for the next 40 years. Pick up and delivery were part of their service. Downtown liveries stabled the horses for the laundry's vehicles (parked in the "Truck Loading Zone"). The number of liveries had decreased from 13 in 1900 to four at the time of this photograph.

Between the end of the Civil War (1865) and the beginning of the Great Depression (1929), America converted itself from a largely rural to a largely urban nation. In the process, modest-sized towns all over the country acquired urban trappings, among them, at least one palatial hotel in the downtown area, which became the unofficial center of social life in the newly created city, the place where the city's power brokers gathered to drink, to dine and to entertain visitors. The architecture of these downtown hotels originated in Chicago and New York, the acknowledged capitals of commercial architecture in the United States. The Tutwiler, shown in this c.1920 photograph, was virtually identical to dozens of similar elite downtown hotels all over the country. To any sophisticated visitor, The Tutwiler was a tangible sign that Birmingham was a city to be taken seriously. *P.L.*

The Tutwiler Hotel (1914-70), Looking South on 20th St. at Fifth Ave. North, c.1920, Birmingham View 43985. After the completion of the Terminal Station in 1909, four hotels, the Tutwiler, the Molton, the Bankhead and the Redmont, rose along Fifth Avenue, raising the number of downtown hotel rooms to 2,797 by 1925. The grandest of the hotels was The Tutwiler opened June 15, 1914. Across Fifth Avenue (recently repaved after the removal of the Tidewater streetcar tracks) at the Molton Hotel, jitney drivers cue up for a fare. Note the clustered telephone cable, an indicator of an elaborate telephone system, and the pedestrians, not all of whom observe the newly painted crossings.

Parade Review, President Warren G. Harding (fourth to right of flag), Mrs. Harding (with the fur), Senator Oscar Underwood, Governor Thomas Kilby, City Commission President N. A. Barrett, The Tutwiler Hotel, October 26, 1921, O. V. Hunt. Across the industrial city, thousands of whistles sounded to open Birmingham's 50th Birthday Party. President's Day featured Harding's review of a grand parade. He also gave an address urging racial equality, opened a meeting of the American Cotton Association, laid the cornerstone for a Masonic Temple, helped inaugurate a Birmingham-Southern College president and witnessed a mine rescue demonstration.

Terminal Station, 501 26th St. North, mid 1920s, Birmingham View. Designed in the Beaux Arts style, the buff brick station featured a massive central dome covering the waiting room for white passengers. Twin towers, 130 feet high, flanked the dome and extensive wings housed the "colored" waiting room at one end of the station and baggage and shipping facilities at the other. The entire complex stretched 600 feet along 26th Street. From opening day in 1909 until 1969, this station served as Birmingham's gateway to the world with 98 passenger trains arriving and departing daily at the time this photograph was made. Only the underpass remains today.

First Ave. North, Looking East to the 20th St. Intersection, c.1921, O. V. Hunt. In an amazingly short time, Birmingham's urban look changed from outpost town to that of a booming city. By 1912, all four corners of the First Avenue and 20th Street intersection were occupied by office towers of 10 to 16 stories. Proud citizens touted the intersection as the "Heaviest Corner on Earth." By the early 1920s, when this photograph was made, streetcars were vying for space with an ever-expanding number of automobiles. Also located on the major east-west thoroughfare pictured here are Porter Clothing and then newly opened Brittling's Cafeteria.

In 1925, popular entertainment in America was at a watershed in time. The Loew's Temple marquee reflects both past and future. The past was live, legitimate theater: vaudeville and a real pipe organ, here, a minstrel show and "4 Other Great Loew Acts," all presumably live. The future was motion pictures, which were still silent when this photograph was taken, requiring "Josef Stoves at the Big Organ" to produce the sound. But things were changing fast. Two years after this photograph was taken, "talking pictures" would arrive on the scene with Al Jolson's *The Jazz Singer*, and vaudeville would gradually pass into history along with minstrels, silent movies and live organ music. A few decades later, TV and the move away from the city center would put downtown movies out of business altogether. *P.L.*

Loew's Temple Theatre (1922-70), Masonic Temple, 517 19th St. North, 1925, Birmingham View 28288. This white granite structure, built in the Classical Revival style, originally housed administrative offices for the Masons, a small theater and an auditorium for Zamora shrine ceremonies. In 1925, Loew's Theatre company converted the auditorium into a vaudeville theater. The Temple also featured movies and such theatrical stars as Alabama's Tallulah Bankhead, Helen Hayes and Katherine Hepburn. It remained the city's premier performance hall for opera and concerts until the construction of the Birmingham-Jefferson Civic Center in the 1970s. AmSouth-Harbert Plaza now occupies the site. The residence pictured in the photograph was demolished in the late 1920s. AmSouth banking, retailing and other professional business take place, here, today.

Play Period, Unidentified City School, c.1926, Birmingham View 28027. By the 1920s, many city schools included large, well-lighted and ventilated "playrooms." The large banks of multi-paned industrial windows provide illumination and ventilation. Such multi-purpose rooms were used for physical education instruction and for special programs. Dressed in dark bloomers and sailor blouses, these young ladies are doing a dancing exercise, probably rehearsing for the annual May Festival. Boys played basketball (at the other end of the room) and participated in track meets. The room also served as a stage.

Central Library-Birmingham Public (now Linn-Henley Research) Library, 2020 Park Place, Opening Day, April 11, 1927, Birmingham View 30845. After a 1925 fire destroyed the library and its books, Birmingham voters authorized a $650,000 bond issue for this classically styled limestone structure, the second municipal building located on today's Linn Park. An art gallery and auditorium occupied the top two floors. Inscriptions, noting names of great artists, scientists and philosophers, indicate the library's role in the transmission of knowledge. Today, this building houses the Birmingham Public Library Archives and Southern History Collections.

Hose Company No. 16, 1621 Avenue G, Ensley, 1927, Birmingham View 40547. During the late 1920s, the City upgraded fire protection in residential areas, completing 24 fully equipped, professional stations. Ensley, East Lake, Southside, Avondale, West End and Woodlawn all received new stations, neighborhood-friendly in design. This Spanish style station included space for the hose cars and other equipment, an office and temporary housing for the firefighters. Originally, the u-shaped station also housed the street and police departments and a jail. Street trees are limed to keep pests away.

The shotgun house is one of the most distinctive features of the traditional Southern landscape. Its form is simple: long and narrow, one-story high, gable end facing front, with single rooms arranged in a row from front to back, connected by doors, but usually with no corridor. Thus, a person entering the house from the front, must pass through one or more other rooms to reach the back. According to legend, the house got its name from the notion that a shotgun fired into the front entrance would exit the rear without hitting a thing. The legend does not explain why anyone would do such a thing, but stories of this sort have great staying power.

The shotgun house is the only common American folk house whose design apparently originated in Africa. The scholar John Vlach traces its American origins to New Orleans in the early 19th century, when it was introduced by free blacks from Haiti, refugees from a murderous war of independence. Those Haitians, Vlach believes, had inherited the design from their ancestral homelands on the slave coast of West Africa.

During the first half of the 19th century, shotgun houses were built in large numbers over much of the South to provide very cheap housing for plantation hands, factory workers or, as here, furnace workers. The shotgun was a very common house in poor districts of Southern towns. In cities like New Orleans and Mobile, shotguns were highly decorated and a step above "poor." They usually served as residential quarters, although the one in the foreground has been converted into a school. *P.L.*

Unidentified School, c.1928, Birmingham View 44619.
Friends share the job of pumping well water in a dirt schoolyard. (Note the pipe that makes this a fountain trough!) In sparsely populated rural areas surrounding Birmingham, individual wells provided water for many homes as late as the 1970s. At low levels of development, groundwater in the limestone bedrock generally yielded adequate quantities of safe drinking water.

Thomas Furnace School, Rear View, c.1923, Birmingham View 88. This orderly group of shotgun houses faces a street at the front of the schoolhouse. The two-room board and batten houses, set on brick piers, have porches on the front and city water at a barrel tap in the rear. Yards of swept dirt are fenced. A 1923 report recommended abandonment of this city school. Similar one-room, one-teacher schools operated in rented or church-owned facilities in rural and mining communities surrounding Birmingham until the 1950s, many of them led by dedicated teachers who instilled solid skills and good behavior in their students.

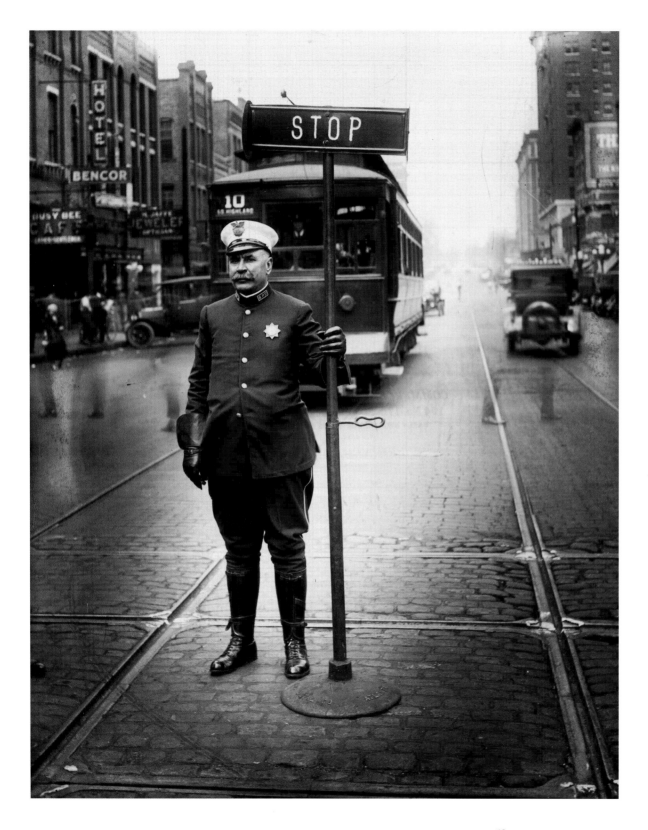

The photographs on the facing and following pages represent a new use of public schools for the welfare of children and young people. Until the time when these photographs were taken, schooling was largely concerned with academic subjects: reading, arithmetic, geography, rhetoric, history. Children from poor families, or those who were destined for manual work, were simply ignored. They were expected to drop out of school at an early age. If children got sick, that was seen as a personal problem and no concern of society at large.

With the rise of the Progressive Movement in the early 1900s, reformers sought to improve the lot of children, and the schools were used as the main tool to do that (urban reformers were especially zealous). Here, we see aspects of the same educational reform movement. The schools would attend to the needs of children far beyond traditional academic lessons. Children coming from poor families could receive medical attention in the school. Even preventative medicine was available through vaccination and regular physical exams. Also, young men who wanted to become auto mechanics could learn to do their jobs properly, and enjoy the dignity of work well done.

When these pictures of Birmingham city schools were taken, such ideas were widely perceived as revolutionary, even socialistic. One must conclude that at least some people in Birmingham held fairly precocious ideas with respect to the function of public schools. *P.L.*

Police Officer, 300 Block 20th St. North, c. 1920, O. V. Hunt. By the time of this photograph, one in ten persons in Birmingham owned an automobile. Downtown traffic had become a nightmare. Police duties included regulating traffic at intersections. This officer posed so long for the camera's exposure that he appears cross and several pedestrians have crossed 20th Street behind him. By the late 1920s, traffic lights were installed downtown and in many suburban communities.

Medical and Dental Clinic, Temporary Cottage, Lincoln Elementary School, c.1927, Birmingham View 47096. Children pose to illustrate medical and dental examinations, first aid treatment and weighing at a child-size scale. Changes in height and weight are tracked on the charts posted on the lattice dividers. Throughout the 1920s, under a plan recommended by the American Medical Association, a staff of physicians and nurses gave regular physical examinations and advised parents of action needed. Classroom teachers stressed health and cleanliness, conducting daily inspections and toothbrush drills.

Auto-Mechanics Shop, Frame Annex, Paul Hayne Opportunity School, c.1930, Birmingham View 48626. In the 1920s, city schools offered students a variety of vocational training. Paul Haynes offered two-year courses in printing, architectural and mechanical drawing, radio, machine shop, patternmaking, painting and decorating, commercial art, electrical work, salesmanship, tea room and cafeteria management, sewing and auto-mechanics. By 1930, the number of automobiles in the city had skyrocketed to 39,159, opening new careers selling, financing, renting, repairing and servicing these machines.

"City Bus," Alliance School, Western Jefferson County, 1920s, Birmingham View 45032. The White Company of Cleveland, Ohio supplied this 20-passenger bus to the Jefferson County school system, the first local system to bus students. While students dressed up for this photo, riding the bus must have been quite dusty.

Country roads were surfaced with "natural gravel," rock ground down by the passing vehicles. This bus is equipped with truck tires (including a spare) and large fenders (to fend off mud) but no wipers. The teacher is the driver. Service stations and replacement buses were few and far between.

Five Points South, Looking North on 20th St. Across the Circle to the Medical Arts Bldg. (now the Pickwick Hotel), 1932, Birmingham View 49553. Five Points South's richly textured, low-scale buildings, sidewalks, street trees, uniform set backs and brick street give it a distinctive urban character. The eight-story Medical Arts Tower (designed exclusively for physicians, surgeons and pharmacists, now the Pickwick Hotel) opened in 1931. Gilchrist Pharmacy advertises its prescription service. At the Circle, riders wait to catch a trolley. Trolley fare was seven cents.

Hillman (now University of Alabama at Birmingham-UAB) Hospital, 600 20th St. South, Early 1930s, Birmingham View 52704. Established in 1897, the hospital opened in 1903 at this location to serve paying patients. A 1907 contract with Jefferson County specified use of the facility "for the purpose of conducting a free charity, non-sectarian hospital." A year later, Hillman became a teaching hospital. In 1930, the hospital's staff of 275 persons treated 298 patients daily. These men and women may be lined up to receive free medical treatment or to apply for a job with Dr. Judson David Dowling, the city-county health officer (1917-1942), who commissioned this photograph.

Gardening Class, Alabama Fuel and Iron Company Co. Mining Camp, St. Clair County, Early 1930s, Birmingham View 50145. Beginning in the 1910s, several area industries offered workers and their families instruction in farming, gardening and canning, and furnished company land for their use. One 1920 estimate notes 17,000 workers living in company housing. Some company built camps included well planned company and community facilities, commissaries, churches, schools and teacher cottages, all located about a central park. Often, these parks included baseball diamonds, as baseball was the preferred game for leisure hours.

The Industrial Revolution of the 19th and early 20th centuries created a whole new world of technology and corporate organization. Everything was bigger, much more impersonal, and socially much more segmented. Huge new corporations invented new ways to improve the efficiency of production, but the social and political methods to deal fairly with disputes between workers and managers lagged far behind. Thus, during the early days of the Industrial Revolution, the old personal relationships between worker and manager had disappeared, but nobody had yet invented peaceful ways to settle labor disputes between classes of people who rarely saw or spoke to one another. In the absence of discourse, disputes often turned violent, especially during hard times when large numbers of men were fired or had their wages cut. From 1934 to 1936, with a deepening depression, the whole United States was swept with an unprecedented wave of violent strikes, and an industrial center like Birmingham was a prime place for such violence. *P.L.*

Strike Damage, Alabama Fuel and Iron Co. Automobile, May 17, 1934, Birmingham View 50693. Between 1881 and 1936, Alabama coal miners initiated 603 strikes, including many in the 1930s. Jefferson County unemployment had reached 32 percent by 1930. Coal and iron production plummeted. As conditions worsened, local coal operators refused to negotiate miners' grievances with national unions. A February 1934 strike involved 2,000 employees at seven mines. Picketing, demonstrations, armed marches and strikes continued into 1939, when 20,000 miners struck for 47 days, shutting down the entire Alabama coal mining industry.

Royal Cup Coffee Delivery Fleet, Batterton Coffee Co. General Offices, 2401 First Ave. North, 1937, Birmingham View 53605. International Harvester Co. commissioned this photograph to record the sale of these snazzy panel trucks, pictured with uniformed deliverymen. A decidedly regal corporate logo is emblazoned on the side panels of each truck. Organized in 1896 to roast and sell coffees, the Batterton business branched out in the 1920s and 1930s, also selling tea, extracts, spices, cocoa and the "Royal Cup" brand of coffee, which became the company name in 1957. This First Avenue building remains.

Lumberyard, Grayson Lumber Co., 715 39th St. North, 1937, Birmingham View.
From 1934 to 1976, Claude H., James M. and Gertie Grayson operated this family firm in East Birmingham, providing building materials, paints, roofing and mill-work to area builders and individuals. This photograph shows three shiny new International tractor-trailers loaded for delivery. At this yard, lumber is cut to size and hand-loaded using the iron-wheeled yard trucks. Grayson Lumber Co. was one of 28 retail lumber dealers in Birmingham, many of whom supplied Alabama forest products. This lumber appears destined for floor joists.

This scene in the Birmingham Board of Education Office, c.1934, is revolutionary for the time, and a harbinger of things to come. The women, with their modern bobbed hair and fashionable dresses, are emancipated wage-earners on their way to freedom in an otherwise male-dominated society. The office environment is modern, too, with its custom-built file cabinets capable of organizing large volumes of data, a precursor of today's computers. *P.L.*

Bathers, East Lake Park, Early 1930s, O.V. Hunt. This unidentified young lady wears a modest, one-piece bathing suit of wool or cotton knit trimmed with striped material. Her suit is accessorized with bathing socks and rubber slippers and cap. The boys wear one-piece suits with rounded neck and shoulders. East Lake, fed by the cool springs which rise in the Roebuck area, was a refreshing and popular swimming hole.

Administrative Offices, Birmingham Board of Education, 2030 Seventh (Park) Ave. (site of current offices), c.1934, Birmingham View 51470. In 1926, school superintendent Charles Glenn set up offices in a house that belonged to the Caheen family. Here, his staff kept records in the bound volumes and filing cabinet pictured. Office furnishings included wooden chairs, desks set with pens and ink blotters, a single telephone and a limited amount of paper. An image of the newly completed Norwood School (1926) hangs from the picture molding. It's springtime, windows are open and flowers deck the room.

WKBC Radio Broadcasting Studio, The Tutwiler Hotel, 2001-05 Fifth Ave. North, c.1932-34, Birmingham View 49638. Radio audiences grew steadily through the 1920s and into the 1930s. With money tight, unemployment still high and television not yet established, radio brought news and entertainment into the home. The city's early commercial broadcasts emanated live from downtown office buildings and hotels. Between musical selections, most local stations placed talk programs with popular personalities telling children's stories, teaching cooking and giving advice.

Junior Chamber of Commerce King and Queen Ball, Municipal (now Boutwell)
Auditorium, 1930 Eighth Ave. North, Late 1930s, Birmingham View 50705.
Organized in 1922 to promote the city's economic development, these civic boosters
(known as the JayCees since the 1960s) also partied, royally. A stage backdrop sets
the tone for the assembled crowd. A big band plays and most couples dance
(two-step and waltzes), some too fast for the camera's slow shutter speed. Some
socialize. Food and drink are not in evidence.

Chinese first came to the United States in large numbers during the late 19th century when male workers were imported as cheap labor to build railroads. Many of those workers sought better pay and greater independence by starting their own businesses, performing services that American men disdained as "women's work," washing clothes and cooking food. By 1900, Chinese laundries and Chinese restaurants were flourishing institutions in the new towns of the West and South where newly built railroads had brought booming populations and booming prosperity. In the South and rural West, where residents traditionally took meals at home, Chinese often ran some of the only reliably inexpensive restaurants in town. Here in Birmingham, Joy Young's with its "private booths" and air conditioning was a popular meeting and eating place for decades.

The menu offerings in such restaurants were typically eclectic. Chop suey was not originally Chinese, but was invented in America to suit American tastes. Thus, while Chinese restaurants offered Americans their first contact with ethnic food, most Chinese restaurateurs hedged their bets by offering both a Chinese and an American menu. *P.L.*

Joy Young Restaurant, 412 20th St. North, c.1937, Birmingham View. Assisted by a wealthy Mobile family, Mansion Joe ("Mr. Joe") and several other Chinese immigrants from Canton, China, established this eatery in 1920. Four years later, the business moved to this location across the street from The Tutwiler, where it remained until 1980. A 1935 remodelling air-conditioned the cafe and created this trendy storefront with its vibrant neon signage. Today, Henry Joe, Mansion Joe's grandson, operates Joy Young's Famous Egg Rolls in Pelham, Alabama. SouthTrust Bank occupies this site, today.

Theater Row, Second Ave. North bet. 19th and 20th Streets (now site of SouthTrust Bank), 1937, Jimmy Wilson, Birmingham View. From the turn of the century through the 1950s, Birmingham's Broadway found its audiences. Long after the lunch hour, the excitement of shopping store to store and going to the theater kept patrons coming downtown. The goods and services they wanted were here. Marquees and signs announced store and theater names and purposes. To make sure nobody missed the message, chaser lights trimmed these elaborate signs. The skyscrapers at First Avenue North and 20th Street tower behind this lively district.

65

Bradford Funeral Home, 1525 Seventh Ave. North, Early 1930s, Cloud Studio. Ersie Bradford conducted his undertaking business in several locations downtown from 1908 until 1941. His Depression-era mortuary was located in this wonderful 1910 residence which combines elements of historic styles, including classical columns, a Romanesque stone arch, Queen Anne gables and an Italianate roof, with cheerful results. The hearse is a Cadillac-based Owen 945, equipped with a full-length flower tray above the casket compartment. In 1926, Cadillac had entered the relatively small but profitable and prestigious market for hearses.

Buckeye Feed and Grain Co., 2325 Morris Ave., January 16, 1938, O. V. Hunt. In 1926, Roy R. Carlisle became district manager for Buckeye Cotton Oil Co. The name appears in scrolled signage on this store, which opened in 1903. The firm sold products made from cotton seed oil until the early 1930s when the Carlisle family, Roy, Roy, Jr., Joshie, J. D. and Frank, turned Buckeye's into a regionally popular wholesaler of food and farm staples. Folks came to town to "Pay Cash & Pay Less" for hay and 100-pound sacks of livestock feed, seed and sugar. Traces of these small town-in-the-city markets can still be found at J. T. Massey Mercantile on Second Avenue North.

The creators of this school display from 1931 clearly believed that leisure activities should be more than fun. Leisure could and should be managed to produce virtue.

This sort of thinking was not peculiar to Birmingham. In the early 20th century, an unlikely combination of engineers, factory managers and social reformers had been promoting the idea that our day-to-day life could be made better by "human engineering," the application of "scientific principles" to ordinary domestic activities. Industrialist Henry Ford, among others, subscribed to this idea. Everything from the shape of coal shovels to the floor plans of kitchens was redesigned to reduce wasted time and motion, and to promote efficiency and increased human productivity. In school, girls no longer learned mere cooking but instead were taught "domestic science." Boys didn't take "shop." Instead, they received "manual training." In the same scientific spirit, leisure was not seen as wasted time, but instead as serving high moral purpose, if designed according to rules discovered by scientists. One concludes from this display that the Birmingham Public Schools stood ready to help children achieve that happy state. *P.L.*

Vulcan Statue and Monument, Red Mountain, Late 1930s, O. V. Hunt. This photograph captures the symbolic placement of the Vulcan statue atop the iron ore vein that supplied the city's industries. From 1860 to 1960, ore was mined from the seam (exposed bottom right) at more than 100 mines along Red Mountain's northern flank. The slender monument, built of limestone rock quarried nearby, featured a floodlit statue, an open air balcony (for viewing the statue and the city) and a museum of minerals (at the base). Completed in 1938, the tower fit superbly into its natural setting and provided visitors grand views of the city.

THE DEVELOPMENT OF CHARACTER THROUGH THE WORTHY USE OF LEISURE
BIRMINGHAM PUBLIC SCHOOLS

Display, Art Gallery, Birmingham Public Library, January 1931, Birmingham View. Beginning in 1924, citywide campaigns fostered character education for school-children. Civic clubs and the press adopted the Birmingham School System's annual themes, such as work, thrift, courtesy and service. The 1930-31 slogan encouraged students to develop appropriate habits for their leisure hours, such as using public libraries and the Y.M.C.A., becoming a Boy or Girl Scout or partici-pating in one of the "57 varieties" of school clubs. This photograph shows one-fifth of the display of the results of pursuing character-enriching hobbies.

Championship Basketball Team, Young Men's Hebrew Association (YMHA, forerunner of today's Jewish Community Center). Team Members: front to rear and left to right: Teddy Roobin, Harry Cohen, Taft Epstein, Joe Weintraub, Al Simons (coach), Ike Epsman, Sam Mendelsohn, Abe Jaffee, Jack Luks (manager), Marvin Goldstein, Steve Browdy, Mickey Lubell, Abe Danenberg, c.1930, Birmingham View 48423. These young men played in a city league with teams from Howard College (now Samford University), Birmingham-Southern College, the YMCA and the Boys' Club. They also challenged travelling professional teams including the Boston Celtics.

Pan-Hellenic Sorority, 1930s, Birmingham View. These young women appear to be dressed for an occasion that remains a mystery. The photographer's notes indicate only that they belonged to the sorority that he indicated. Their formal gowns of satin and chiffon accented with laces and flounces, deep berthas, flowing sleeves and drapes pulled to the back of the skirts (and held out by bustles) demonstrate fashions from the 1870s to the 1920s.

Statuette Manufacturer, Unidentified Location, Late 1930s, Birmingham View 53930. The Chamber of Commerce commissioned this photograph which shows men grinding, filing and finishing miniature reproductions of Birmingham's Vulcan statue. In the 1930s, these Vulcan statuettes touted the city's pride and industrial might and popularized the newly created Vulcan Park, then emerging as the region's leading visitor destination. Conceived as an exhibit for the St. Louis World's Fair of 1904, the statue represents the Roman god at his workstation with anvil and hammer, triumphantly holding aloft a spearpoint he has just made.

Marching Band, Parker High School, 500 Eighth Ave. North, Smithfield, Early 1940s, Birmingham View. Directed by Wilton Robertson (left), this award-winning band participated in parades as far away as Detroit and St. Louis. The band's repertoire included spirited renditions of *Stars and Stripes Forever* and *Chicago Tribune*. This Parker Band also played Birmingham native Erskine Hawkins' 1939 hit tune, *Tuxedo Junction*, as a march. Established in 1899, Parker remained the city's only black high school until 1952. Parker's disciplined music program trained many great musicians including the Bascomb Brothers, Joe Jones, Haywood Henry and Sun Ra.

Used Car Lot, Crawford Auto Shop Inc., 1709 Fifth Ave. North, 1937, Birmingham View 54023. For 50 years, the Crawford (later Maring-Crawford) firm sold and serviced Ford automobiles and trucks downtown. In 1917, Edward B. Crawford became "Special Agent Ford Cars." By the 1930s, his firm was also selling used autos and trucks at this lot which backs up to the Fourth Avenue business district. Pictured left to right are rear views of the New Home Hotel, Frolic Theatre, Quality Department Store, the seven-story Masonic Temple and the Thomas Jefferson Hotel. The lot is now the site of the U. S. Courthouse parking lot.

DeBardeleben Coal Company Pay Office and Store, Unidentified Location, 1930s, Birmingham View 55905. In remote coal mining areas, the company store had it all, albeit the selection was limited and the prices set by the company. This terribly tidy store offered canned foods and sewing supplies, pipes and tobacco, lamps, tires and rugs. Two large wall signs advertised that Coca-Cola was also available. The crisply painted store interior was illuminated by schoolhouse lights with pull chains, heated by a pot-bellied, coal-fired stove and cooled by ceiling fans. The floors were oiled to keep down the dust.

These two familiar scenes, in fact, reflect revolutionary innovations both in technology and in corporate marketing, and demonstrate that Birmingham was very much a part of the modern world.

Until fairly recent times, small household items made of metal, glass and cloth were fabricated by hand, by tinkers, glass-blowers and weavers who often worked part-time at their crafts, and sold or traded their products locally. The quality and cost of such goods varied greatly, and the supply was often undependable, too. All that changed in the late 19th century. New machinery allowed mass-production of consumer items from frying pans to flags, from laundry tubs to clothing, at very low cost and dependable quality. At the same time, new marketing techniques were invented to distribute and sell these items, driving many small-scale craftsmen and shopkeepers out of business. S. H. Kress opened the first "5-and-10 cent stores" in New York and Pennsylvania, and they quickly spread across the country in national "chains" which peddled cheap, standardized items in vast quantities. The first Kress store in Birmingham opened in 1899. Another marketing innovation was the department store, where all sorts of consumer items were organized into "departments" and sold under the same physical and corporate roof. The idea originated almost simultaneously in New York, Philadelphia and Chicago, soon spread all over the country, and is seen here with "The Parisian," a multi-storied department store opened on 18th Street in Birmingham around 1928. *P.L.*

The Parisian, 300 18th St. North, c.1928, Birmingham View 43352. This locally owned five-story store offered ready-to-wear and dry goods. Designed in the tradition of New York and Chicago department stores, it opened shortly before this photograph was made. On this day, at 10:50 a.m., it appears to be sunny and hot. Expanses of windows are shaded and open. A crowd, principally of ladies dressed in high heels and hats, is gathered at the entrance, a spot well delineated by the towering vertical and horizontal signs. Someone is giving away a Chrysler Plymouth.

C. L. Bromberg Store, 5523 First Ave. North, Woodlawn, 1940s, Birmingham View.
This neighborhood variety store, located next door to the old Woodlawn City Hall, sold an astonishing array of goods priced in the 10-to-39-cent range. Scrub brushes; galvanized tubs, pots, pans and cleansing pads; strainers, bottle caps and corks; lunch boxes and thermoses; paint and paint rollers; books and framed items; pinwheels and trinkets could be purchased and wrapped at the side counter. The store's interior is floored with checkerboard linoleum, lit by fluorescent lights and cooled by an electric fan suspended from the acoustical tile ceiling.

By 1940, when this photograph was taken, railroads had dominated American life for almost a century. Wherever railroads reached in America, they brought new people, new products and new wealth. Railroad companies were among the most powerful corporations in America, and they went to considerable trouble to demonstrate that power in a tangible way. Here, in downtown Birmingham, an L & N steam locomotive wears a "modern" streamlined exterior jacket, a symbol of speed, and modern efficiency, modeled after a new generation of streamlined aircraft. Nobody at the time realized that the railroads were living on borrowed time, much of their freight and passenger traffic soon to be hijacked by trucks, automobiles and even airplanes. Within 20 years, this proudly modern locomotive would be consigned to the scrap heap, an obsolete relic of a bygone time. *P.L.*

Birmingham Municipal Airport Terminal, Looking Toward the Hangar, Birmingham View 48938. Early air passengers received a front porch welcome. Opened in 1931, the city's first municipal airport was located on a 315-acre site, 5 miles and 15 minutes from downtown. "Built on a foundation of hospitality, as an invitation to air commerce," the "sky harbor's" facilities included this stately Southern Colonial style "modern administration building," a hangar and runways. Air travel expanded significantly in the late 1950s, but a high state tax on aviation fuel stinted local growth. This facility was demolished at this time.

Louisville & Nashville (L & N) Railroad Engine 275, 1940, Birmingham View. The L & N played a major role in the early development of the city and the surrounding mineral region. Its passenger station (pointed roof at the left) and freight office (with man in the window) were located on 20th Street at the heart of the city. These rail-related buildings were demolished in the 1960s for construction of the Bank for Savings Building and a parking lot. The early skyscrapers of the Heaviest Corner on Earth (pictured left to right, Woodward Building-National Bank of Commerce, Empire Building-Colonial Bank and John Hand Building) remain.

Birmingham was not alone in possessing slums of the kind shown on the facing page. During the early years of the Industrial Revolution, immigrants thronged to newly booming industrial cities in search of work. Many of the immigrants had to settle for poor-paying jobs and, in the 1930s, to make things worse, the Great Depression would throw more workers out of work. The poor lived wherever they could, in "shanty towns" made of poorly constructed houses and ad hoc structures fabricated from whatever was available, bits of cloth, wood and corrugated iron. Most of these slums sprang up in the vicinity of heavy industry or railroad yards, overcrowded and polluted places seldom frequented by affluent people or health inspectors. Today, most shanty towns have been destroyed as a result of reformers' zeal and industrial shut-downs. *P.L.*

Tom's Real Shine, 1914 Fourth Ave. North, c.1937, O. V. Hunt. Although Tom's is not one of the shoe shiners listed in the city directories in the 1930s, Tom (dressed in white) appears to be an entrepreneurial young man who has attracted a fashionably dressed clientele. His tiny shine shop was well-located at a bus stop (No. 38 to Smithfield) in a high-volume pedestrian area across from the old City Hall and Market and next to an all-day parking lot (25 cents a day). According to Willie Roberts (in the shop door), who was waiting to catch the bus when asked to participate in this photograph, the photograph was staged.

Rear View, Shanty Town, 903-929 22nd Court South, Backyard, Palvado House (1891), 2219 Ninth Ave. South, Looking West, c.1939, Birmingham View 44511. A 1939 tax assessor report describes these saddlebag houses as "Negro Houses on Alley," renting for $15.00 a month. These board and batten structures were built at the rear of a 295 foot deep lot behind a late 19th century house (not pictured). In the center of the photograph, rise the towers of the 13-room Queen Anne-style Erswell House (1890, left) and the Royal Arms Apartments (built as the Quinlan Castle in 1927, right). The site is located to the rear of today's Vogue Cleaners on 23rd Street South.

Broadway, Homewood, May 14, 1941, Birmingham View 57229. Tree-lined Broadway in suburban Edgewood represents the typical American streetcar suburb. Streetcars (from downtown via Five Points South) first arrived here in 1912. Before long, as these suburbanites gain access to automobiles, they will no longer need the trolley for trips to work or shopping downtown. The overhead power line will come down and, the next time the street is repaired, the trolley tracks will be covered with a layer of asphalt. The trolley which created this suburb will disappear into history.

Sloss Furnaces, First Ave. North between 26th and 32nd Streets, View Looking Northwest from Powell Avenue, c.1938, Birmingham View 50670. Iron ore (large pile, left), coke (center) and limestone (right) have been delivered via rail and are being loaded onto conveyors and transported via skip hoists (oblique angle) into the two blast furnaces (the largest vertical structures). From these locally mined minerals, the furnaces produced iron bars (in the open gondola cars) used to make cast iron stoves, cotton gins, steel and, especially, cast iron pipe. Today, these Sloss Furnaces, silent since 1970, fill with vistors, metalworkers and festivals.

Acknowledgements

The creation and publishing of this volume has been assisted by a very large number of individuals.
What follows is a list of the many who have helped, and for whose assistance we are indebted.

FINANCIAL ASSISTANCE
The Daniel Foundation of Alabama
Robert R. Meyer Foundation
The Steiner Foundation
Time Warner Inc.
CPC International Inc.
Gary H. Dobbs, Jr.
Philip A. Morris
Herbert and Jane Longenecker
James H. White, III

PRODUCTION
Design: Scott Fuller, icon graphics
Publication and Exhibit Prints: Melissa Springer
Study Prints: Gary H. Dobbs, Jr.

Research: Marjorie Lee White, Christopher Dennis, assisted by the staffs of the Birmingham Public Library Archives, Southern History and Government Document Departments: Jim Baggett, Archivist; Don Veasey, Curator of Photography, Yolanda Valentin, Yvonne Crumpler, Roger Torbert, Jim Pate, Ron Joullian, Danny Dorroh, Becky Scarborough

Readers: Alice Bowsher, Stewart Dansby, Christopher Dennis, Gary H. Dobbs, Jr., Joe Strickland, James H. White, III, Don Veasey, Marjorie Lee White, Marvin Whiting

Assistance with Photograph Identification: Neal Berte and many others at Birmingham Southern College, Alice Bowsher, Birmingham Fire Department, Helen Cocoris, Don Dodd, Rusty Goldsmith, John Holcomb, Joe Holley, Alvin Hudson, Jefferson County Cooperative Extension Service Agent, Crawford Johnson, Shirley LaRussa, Jane Longenecker, Cindy Lovoy and the Fittings Department of American Cast Iron Pipe Company, J. L.and Roberta Lowe, June Mays, Hugh Morgan, Bode Morin, Richard O'Connor, W. C. Patton, Bill Paxton, Cindy Peyton, Kip Porter, Teddy Roobin, Frances Robb, Bill Smith, Rick Sprague, Paige Wainwright, Jim and Virginia White, Louise Wrinkle

Assistance with Photograph Selection: Gary H. Dobbs, Jr., Tom Ford, Greg Hodges, Randy Lawrence, Emily Jones Rushing, Marvin Whiting

Birmingham Public Library Exhibit: November 17-December 31, 1996: Anne Knight, Sharon Hill

The Birmingham News Column: November 1996-February 1997: Ray Brown, Carol Nunnelly, Tom Scarritt, Terri Troncale

Promotion: Stewart Dansby, Victor Hansen, III, Carolanne Roberts
Support: Jackie Dobbs, Felicia Lewis
Research and Production Coordination: Marjorie L. White